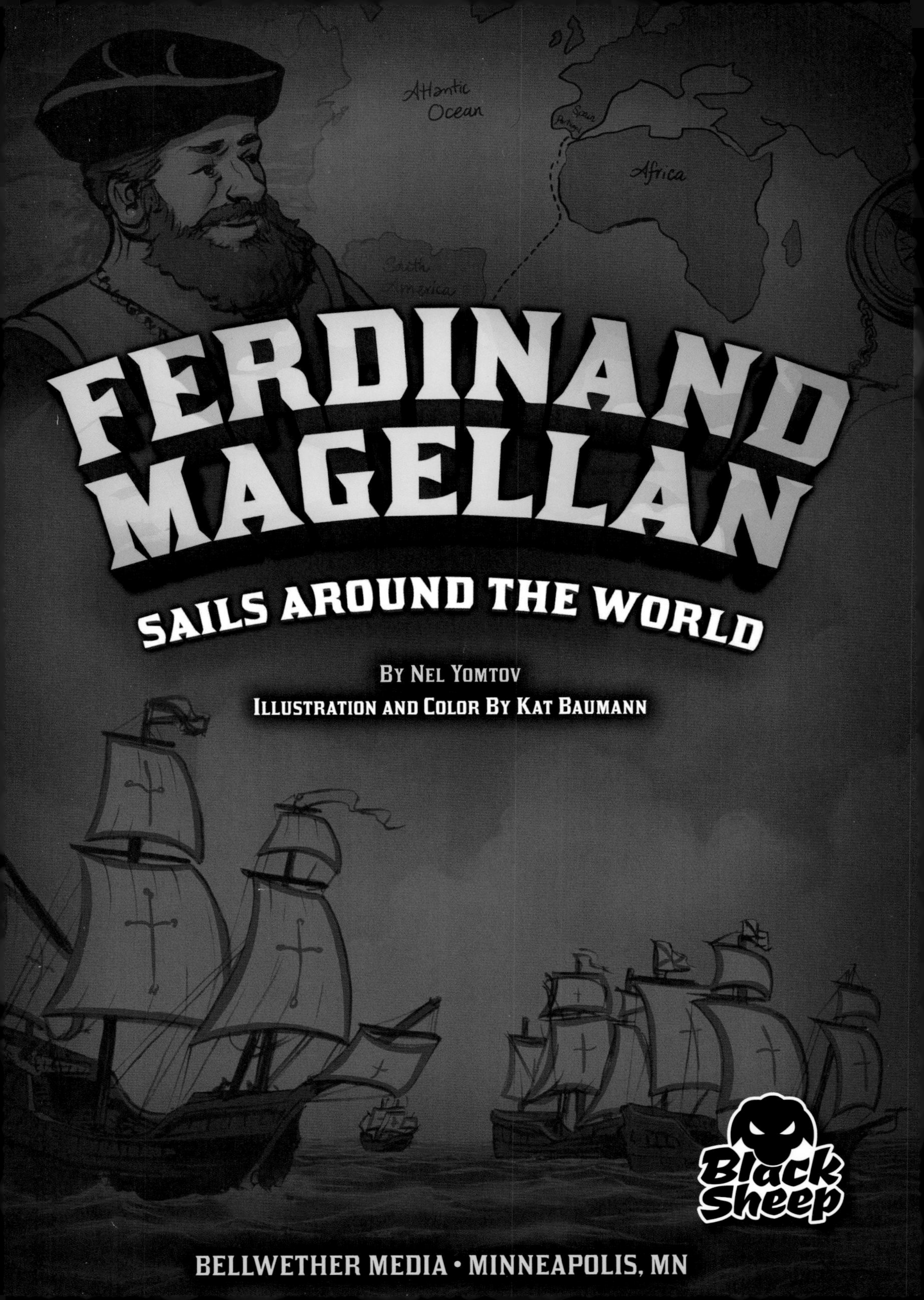
Atlantic Ocean
Spain
Africa
South America

FERDINAND MAGELLAN

SAILS AROUND THE WORLD

By Nel Yomtov
Illustration and Color By Kat Baumann

Black Sheep
BELLWETHER MEDIA • MINNEAPOLIS, MN

STRAY FROM REGULAR READS
WITH BLACK SHEEP BOOKS.
FEEL A RUSH WITH EVERY READ!

Library of Congress Cataloging-in-Publication Data

Yomtov, Nelson.
  Ferdinand Magellan Sails Around the World / by Nel Yomtov.
      pages cm. -- (Black Sheep: Extraordinary Explorers)
  Summary: "Exciting illustrations follow the events of Ferdinand Magellan sailing around the world. The combination of brightly colored panels and leveled text is intended for students in grades 3 through 7"-- Provided by publisher.
  Audience: Ages 7 to 12
  In graphic novel form.
  Includes bibliographical references and index.
  ISBN 978-1-62617-292-0 (hardcover: alk. paper)
  1. Magalhães, Fernão de, -1521--Juvenile literature. 2. Explorers--Portugal--Biography--Juvenile literature. 3. Voyages around the world--Juvenile literature. I. Title.
  G286.M2Y66 2016
  910.4'1--dc23
                              2014050314

This edition first published in 2016 by Bellwether Media, Inc.

Printed in the United States of America, North Mankato, MN.

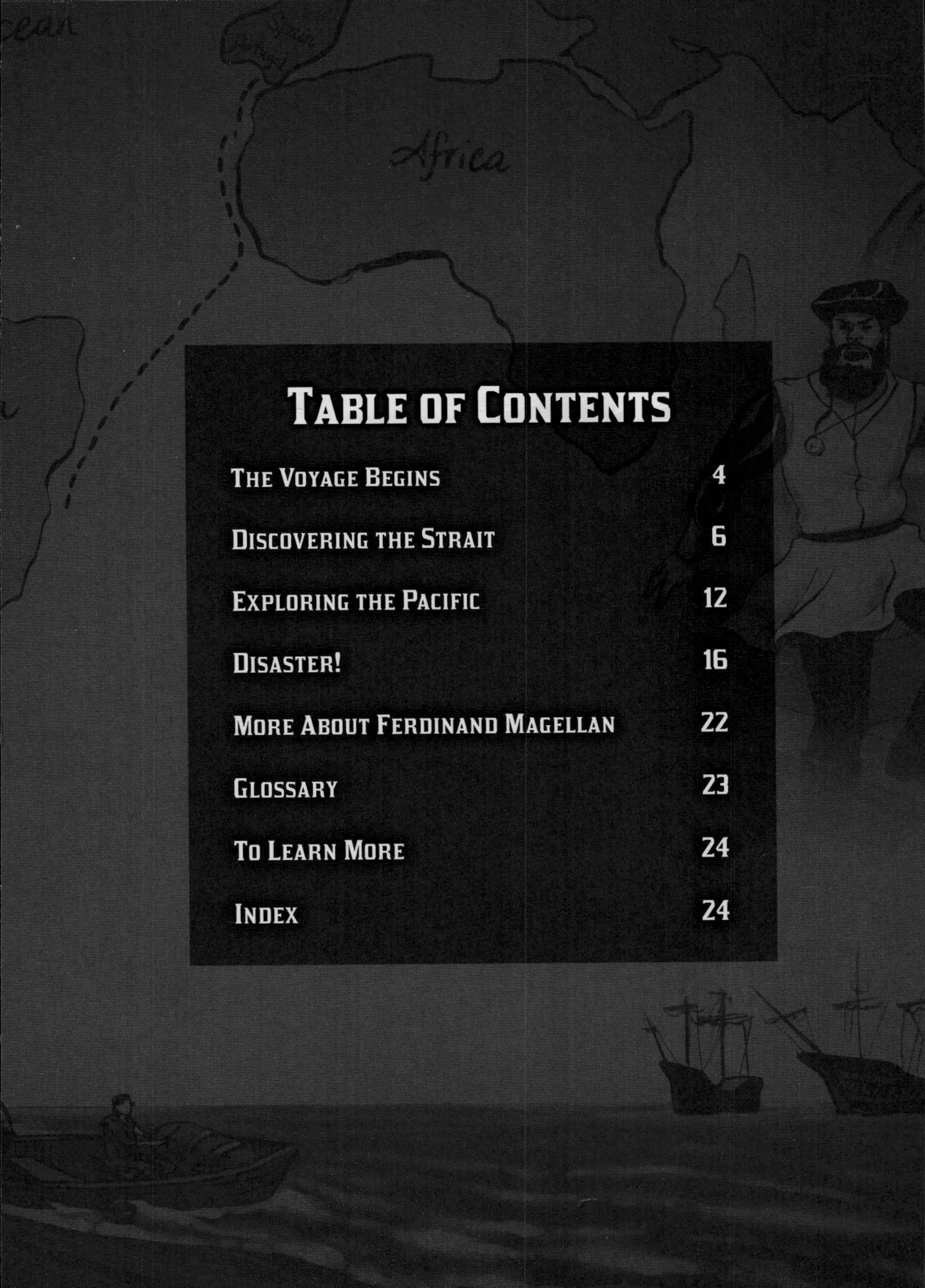
Africa

Table of Contents

The Voyage Begins

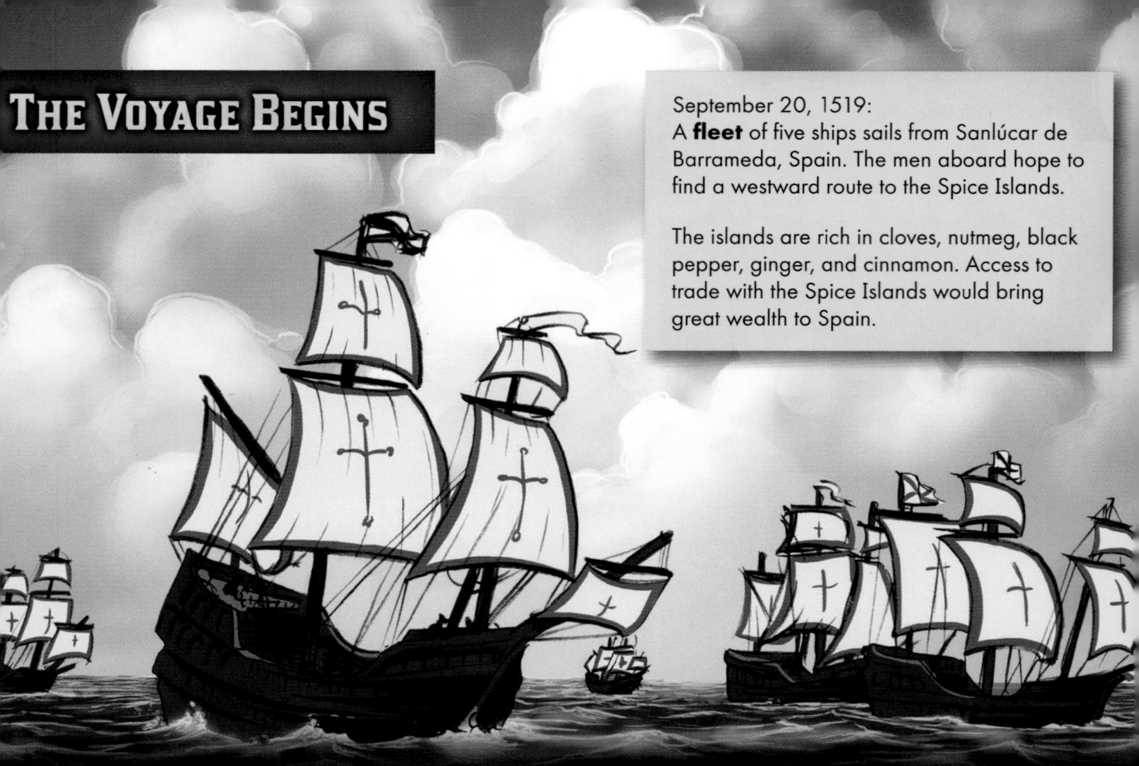
September 20, 1519:
A **fleet** of five ships sails from Sanlúcar de Barrameda, Spain. The men aboard hope to find a westward route to the Spice Islands.
The islands are rich in cloves, nutmeg, black pepper, ginger, and cinnamon. Access to trade with the Spice Islands would bring great wealth to Spain.

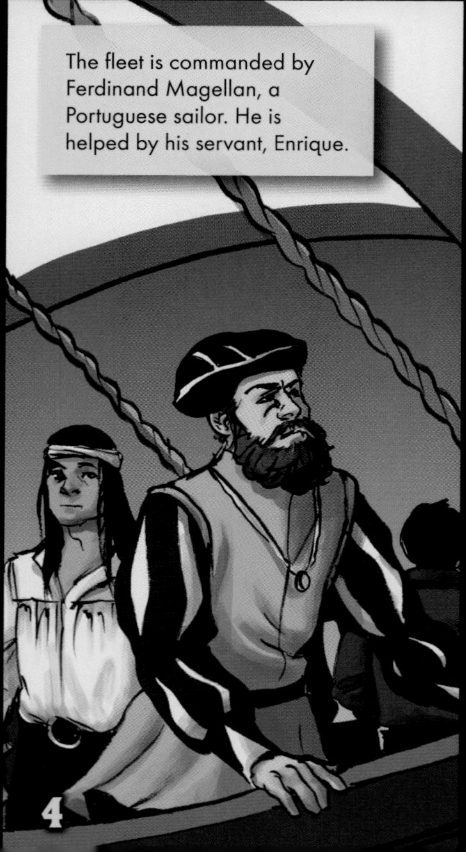
The fleet is commanded by Ferdinand Magellan, a Portuguese sailor. He is helped by his servant, Enrique.

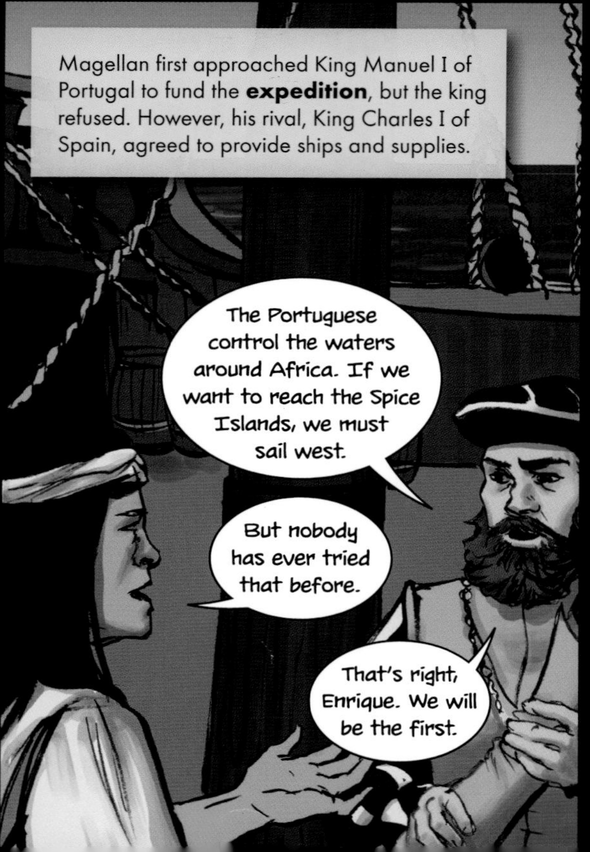
Magellan first approached King Manuel I of Portugal to fund the **expedition**, but the king refused. However, his rival, King Charles I of Spain, agreed to provide ships and supplies.
The Portuguese control the waters around Africa. If we want to reach the Spice Islands, we must sail west.
But nobody has ever tried that before.
That's right, Enrique. We will be the first.

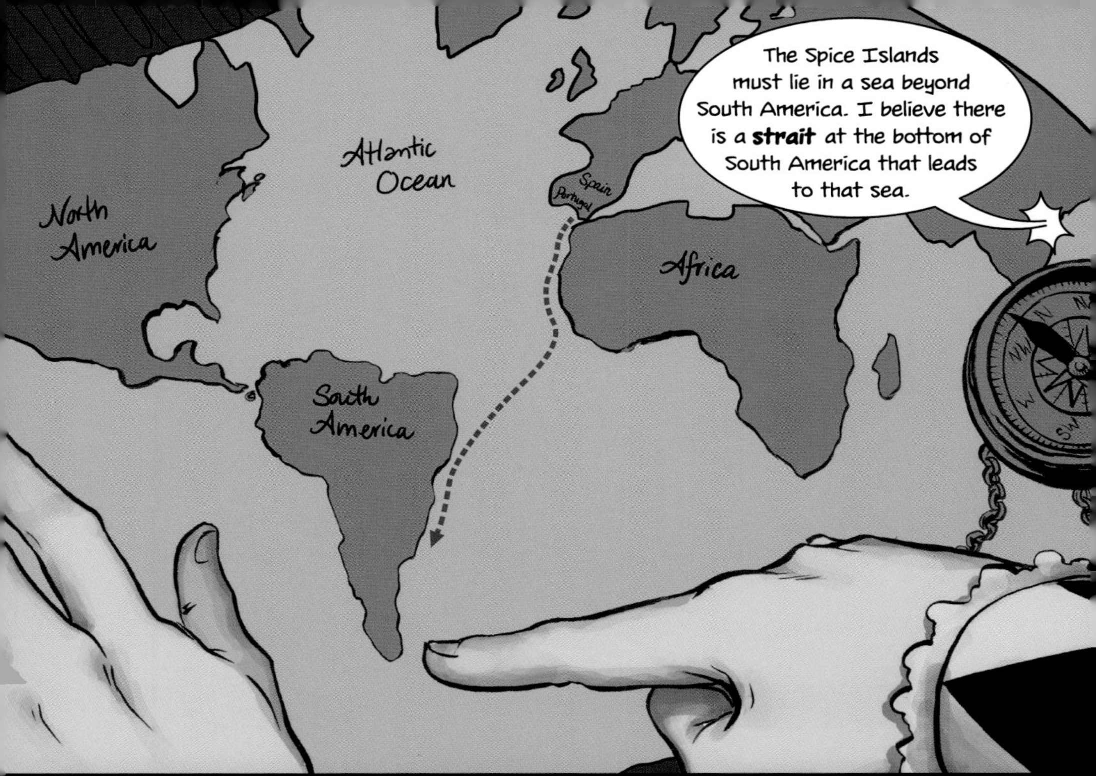
The Spice Islands must lie in a sea beyond South America. I believe there is a **strait** at the bottom of South America that leads to that sea.
Atlantic Ocean
North America
South America
Africa
Spain
Portugal

About 270 men sail on the expedition. Many of the sailors are Spanish or Portuguese.

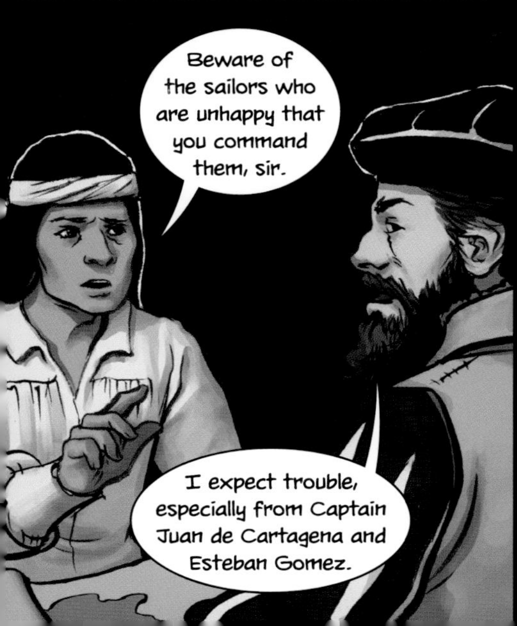
Beware of the sailors who are unhappy that you command them, sir.
I expect trouble, especially from Captain Juan de Cartagena and Esteban Gomez.

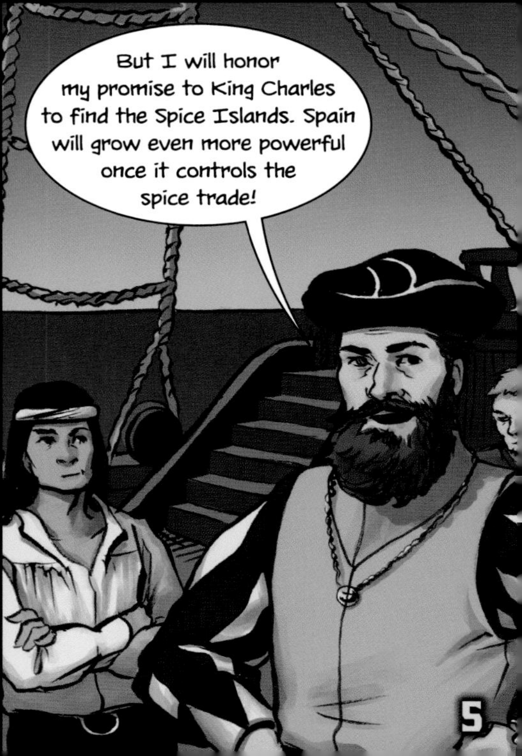
But I will honor my promise to King Charles to find the Spice Islands. Spain will grow even more powerful once it controls the spice trade!

Discovering the Strait

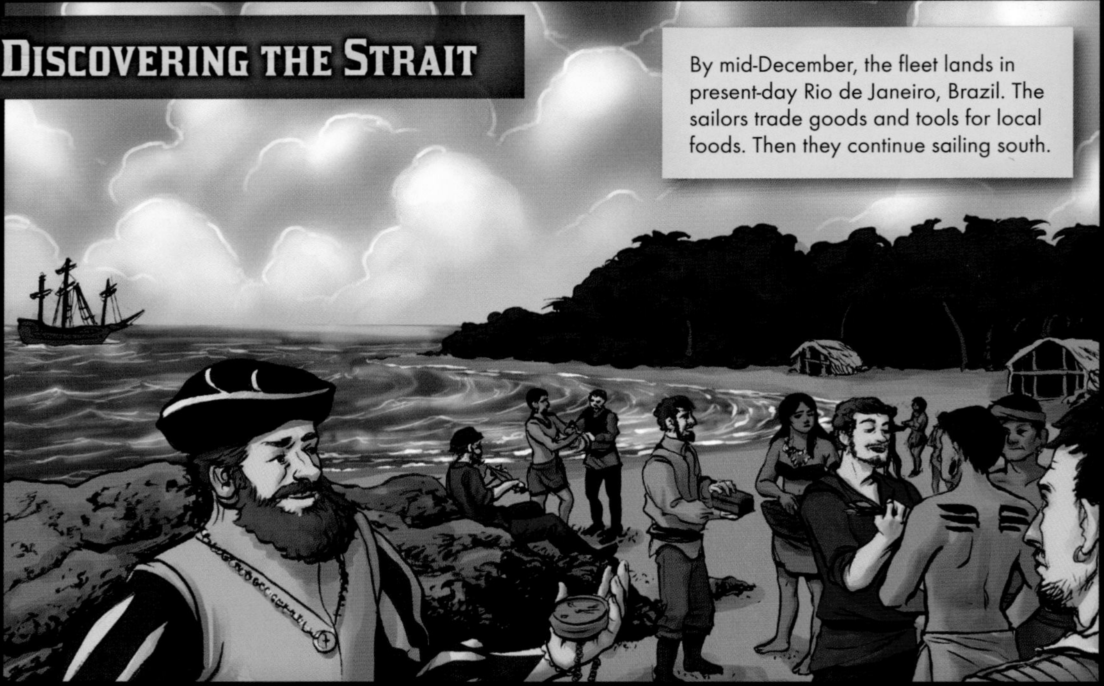

By mid-December, the fleet lands in present-day Rio de Janeiro, Brazil. The sailors trade goods and tools for local foods. Then they continue sailing south.

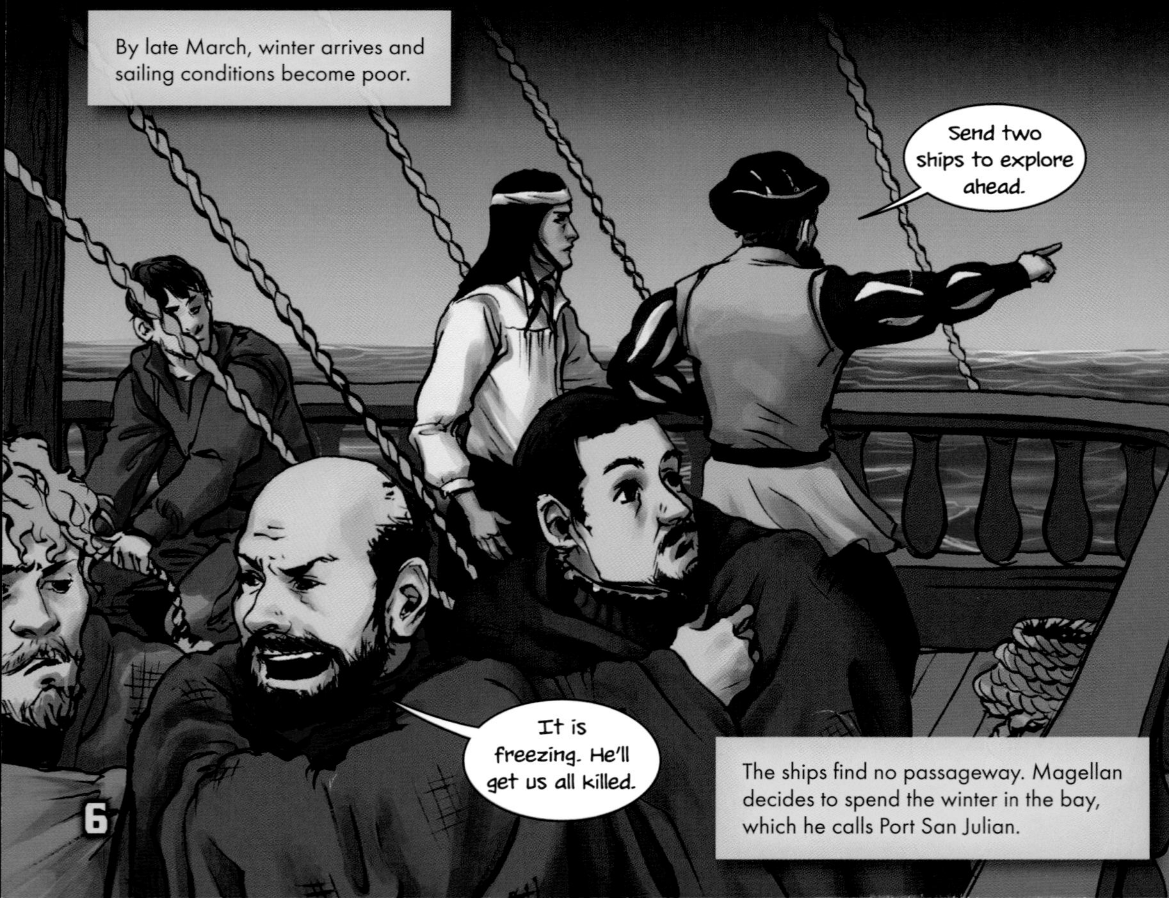

By late March, winter arrives and sailing conditions become poor.
Send two ships to explore ahead.
It is freezing. He'll get us all killed.
The ships find no passageway. Magellan decides to spend the winter in the bay, which he calls Port San Julian.

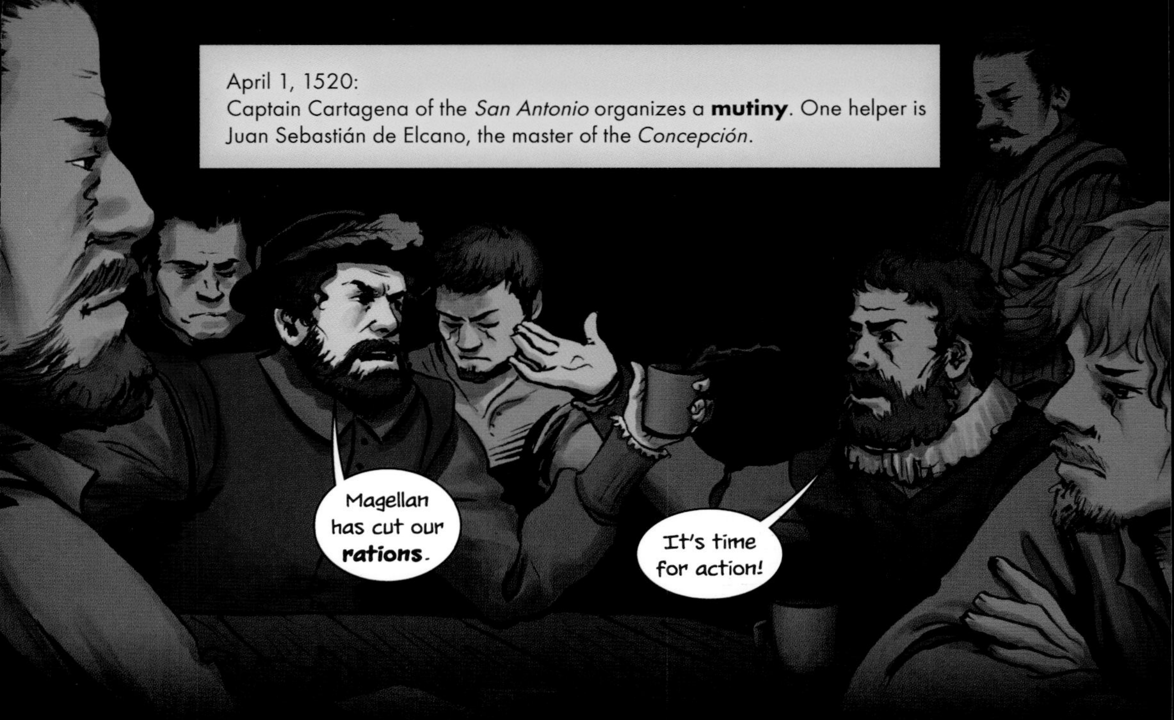
April 1, 1520:
Captain Cartagena of the *San Antonio* organizes a **mutiny**. One helper is Juan Sebastián de Elcano, the master of the *Concepción*.
Magellan has cut our **rations**.
It's time for action!

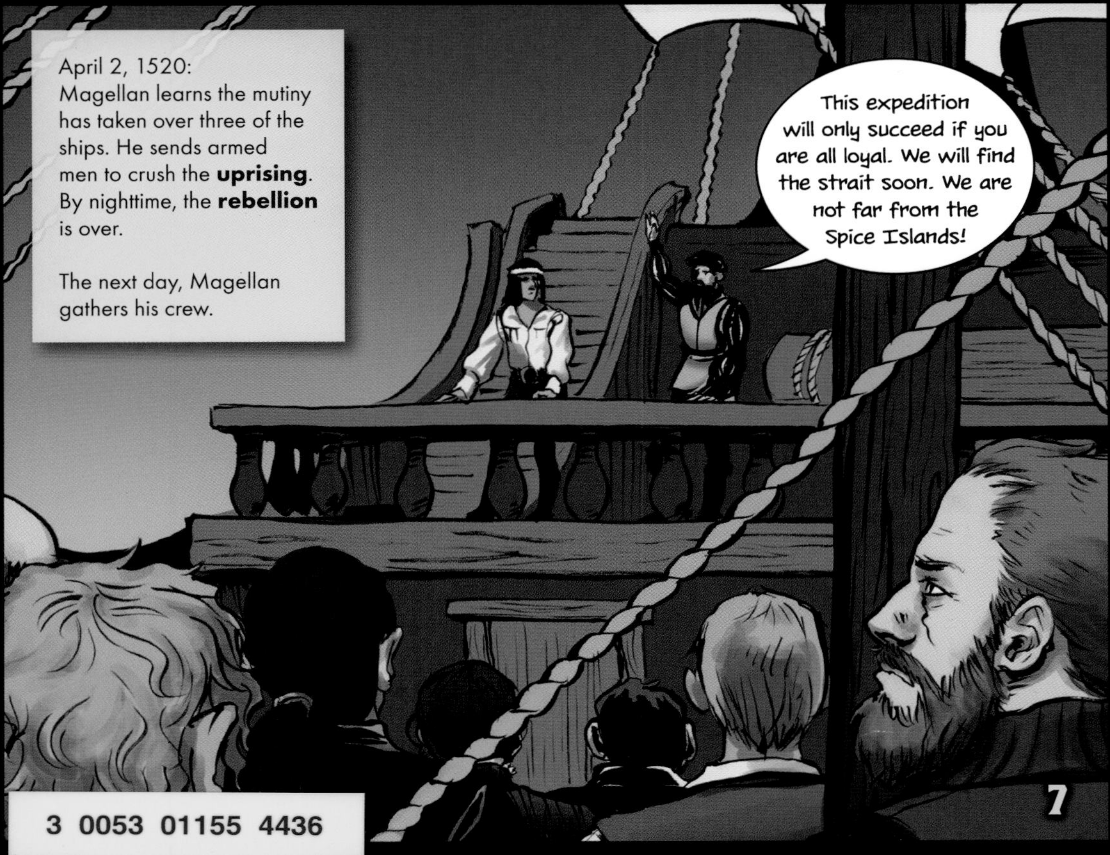
April 2, 1520:
Magellan learns the mutiny has taken over three of the ships. He sends armed men to crush the **uprising**. By nighttime, the **rebellion** is over.
The next day, Magellan gathers his crew.
This expedition will only succeed if you are all loyal. We will find the strait soon. We are not far from the Spice Islands!

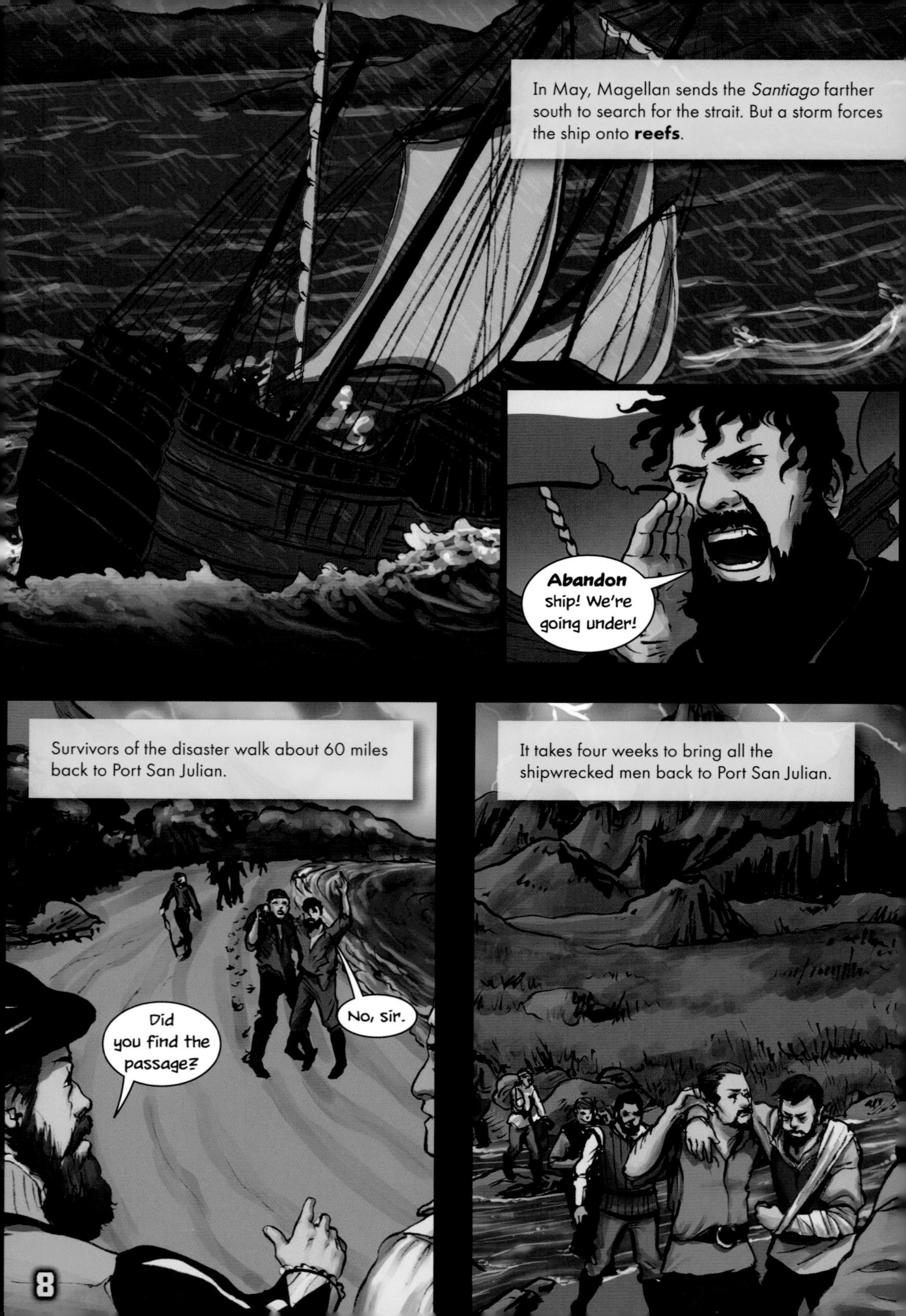
In May, Magellan sends the *Santiago* farther south to search for the strait. But a storm forces the ship onto **reefs**.
Abandon ship! We're going under!
Survivors of the disaster walk about 60 miles back to Port San Julian.
Did you find the passage?
No, sir.
It takes four weeks to bring all the shipwrecked men back to Port San Julian.

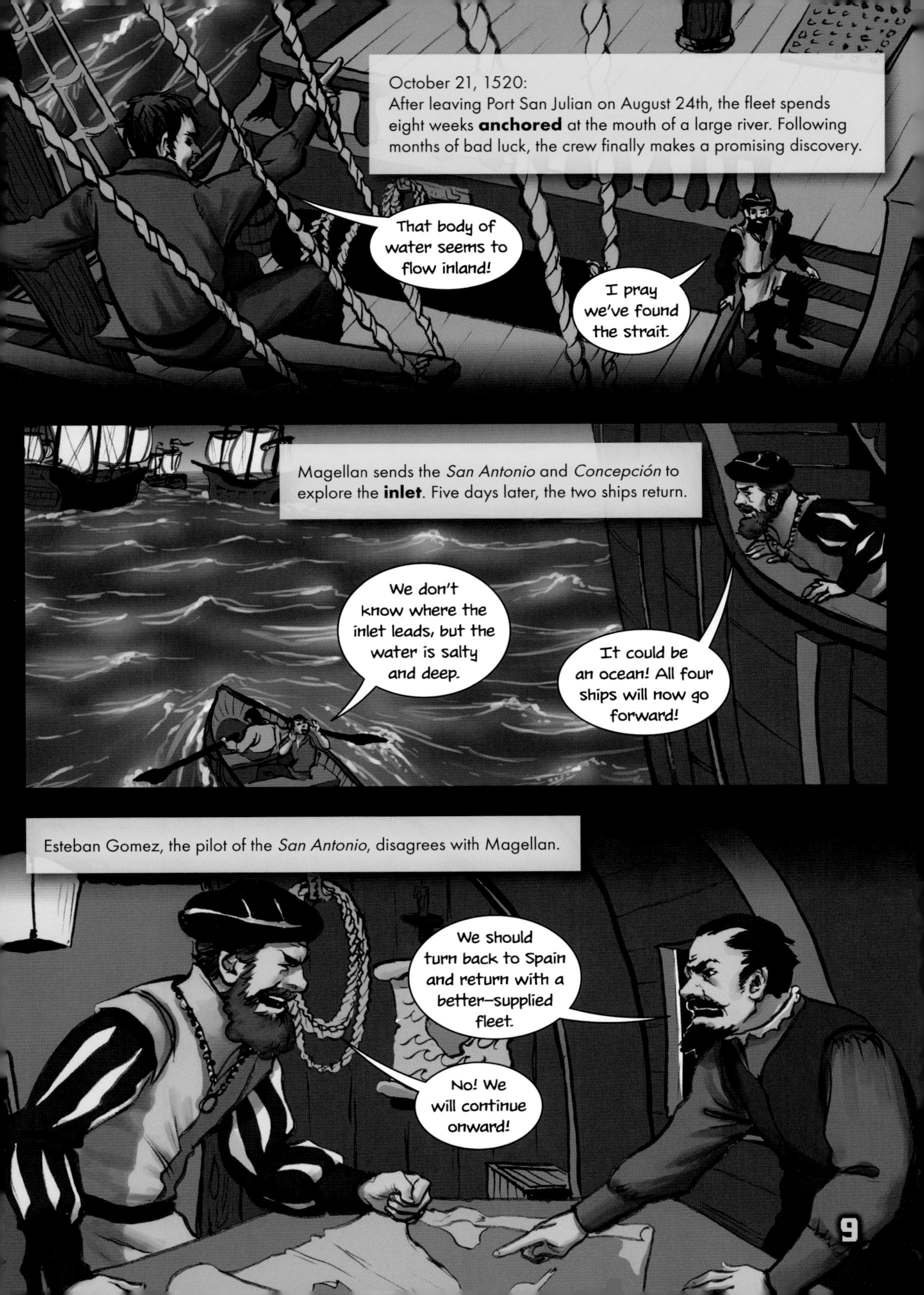
October 21, 1520:
After leaving Port San Julian on August 24th, the fleet spends eight weeks **anchored** at the mouth of a large river. Following months of bad luck, the crew finally makes a promising discovery.
That body of water seems to flow inland!
I pray we've found the strait.
Magellan sends the *San Antonio* and *Concepción* to explore the **inlet**. Five days later, the two ships return.
We don't know where the inlet leads, but the water is salty and deep.
It could be an ocean! All four ships will now go forward!
Esteban Gomez, the pilot of the *San Antonio*, disagrees with Magellan.
We should turn back to Spain and return with a better-supplied fleet.
No! We will continue onward!

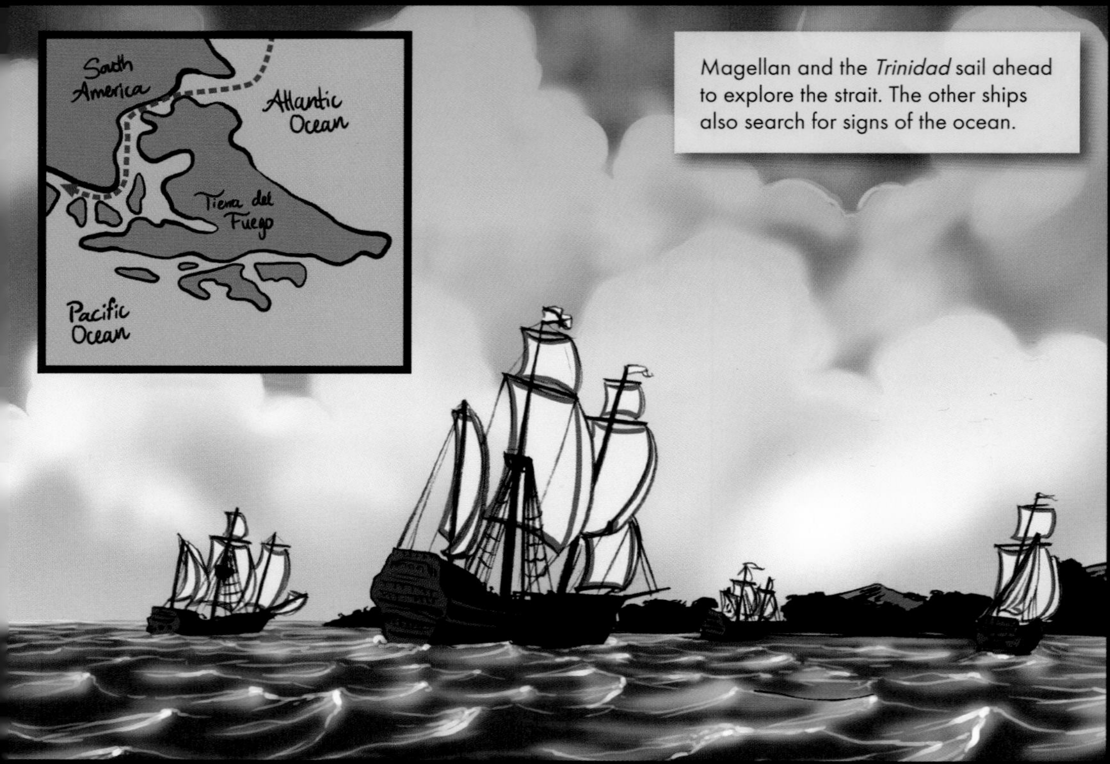
South America
Atlantic Ocean
Tierra del Fuego
Pacific Ocean
Magellan and the *Trinidad* sail ahead to explore the strait. The other ships also search for signs of the ocean.

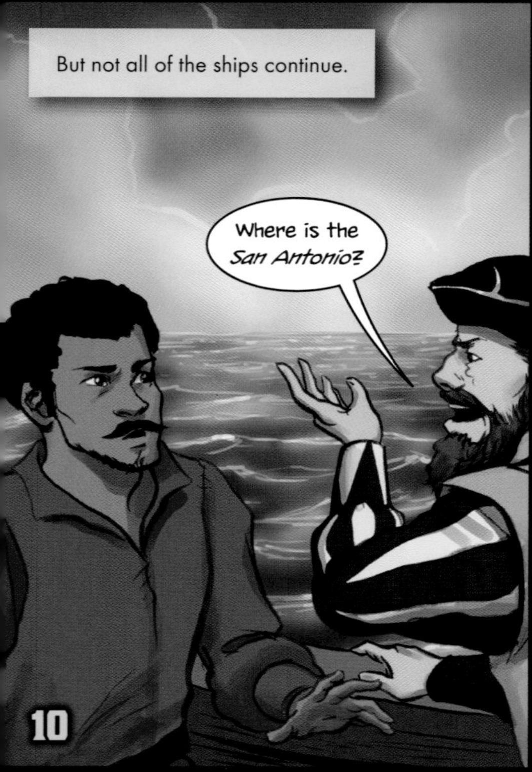
But not all of the ships continue.
Where is the *San Antonio*?

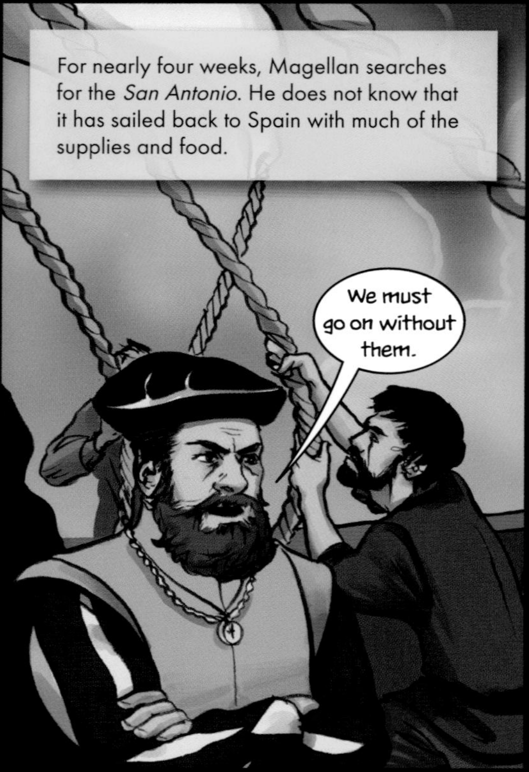
For nearly four weeks, Magellan searches for the *San Antonio*. He does not know that it has sailed back to Spain with much of the supplies and food.
We must go on without them.

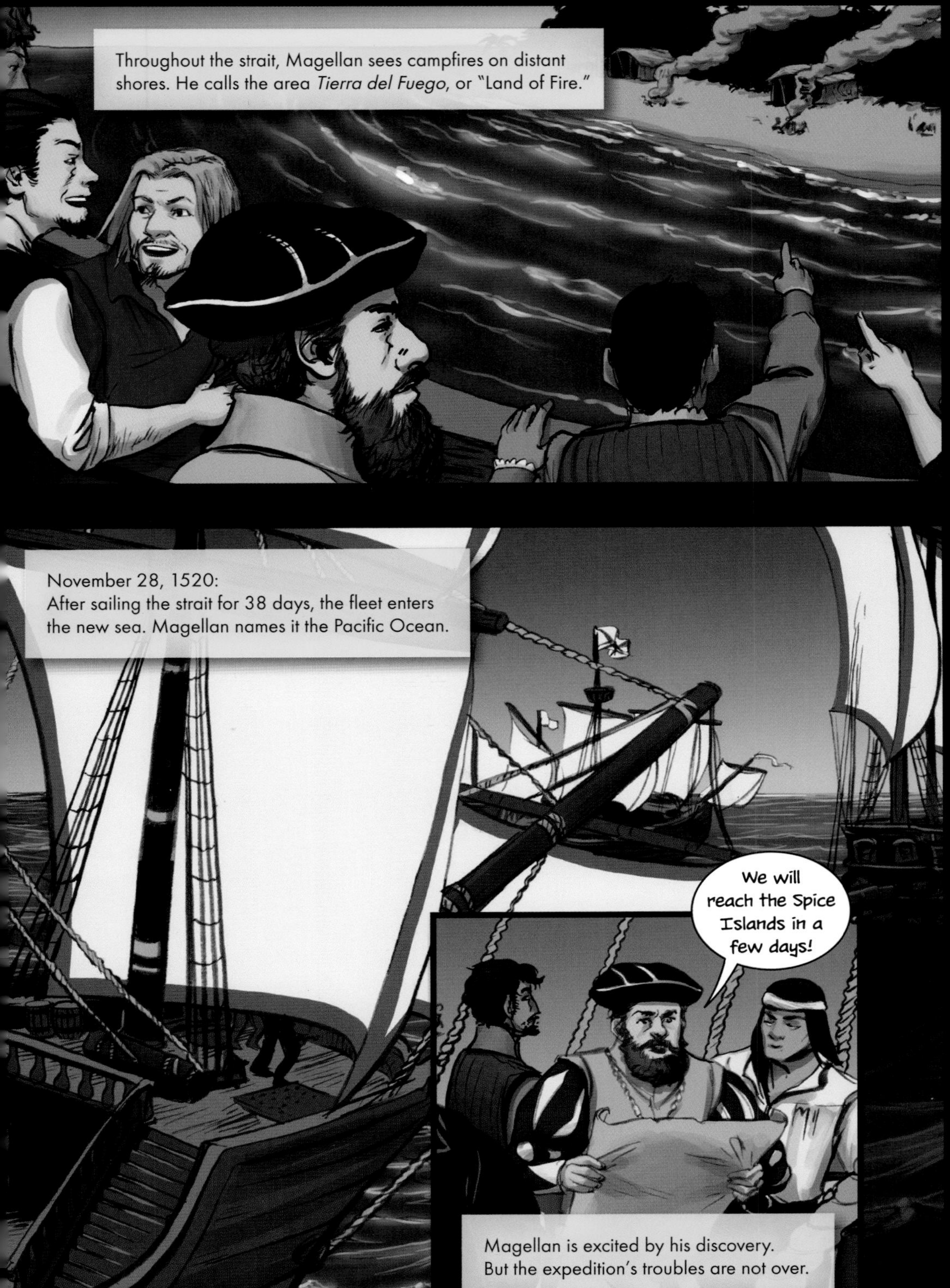
Throughout the strait, Magellan sees campfires on distant shores. He calls the area *Tierra del Fuego*, or "Land of Fire."
November 28, 1520:
After sailing the strait for 38 days, the fleet enters the new sea. Magellan names it the Pacific Ocean.
We will reach the Spice Islands in a few days!
Magellan is excited by his discovery. But the expedition's troubles are not over.

EXPLORING THE PACIFIC

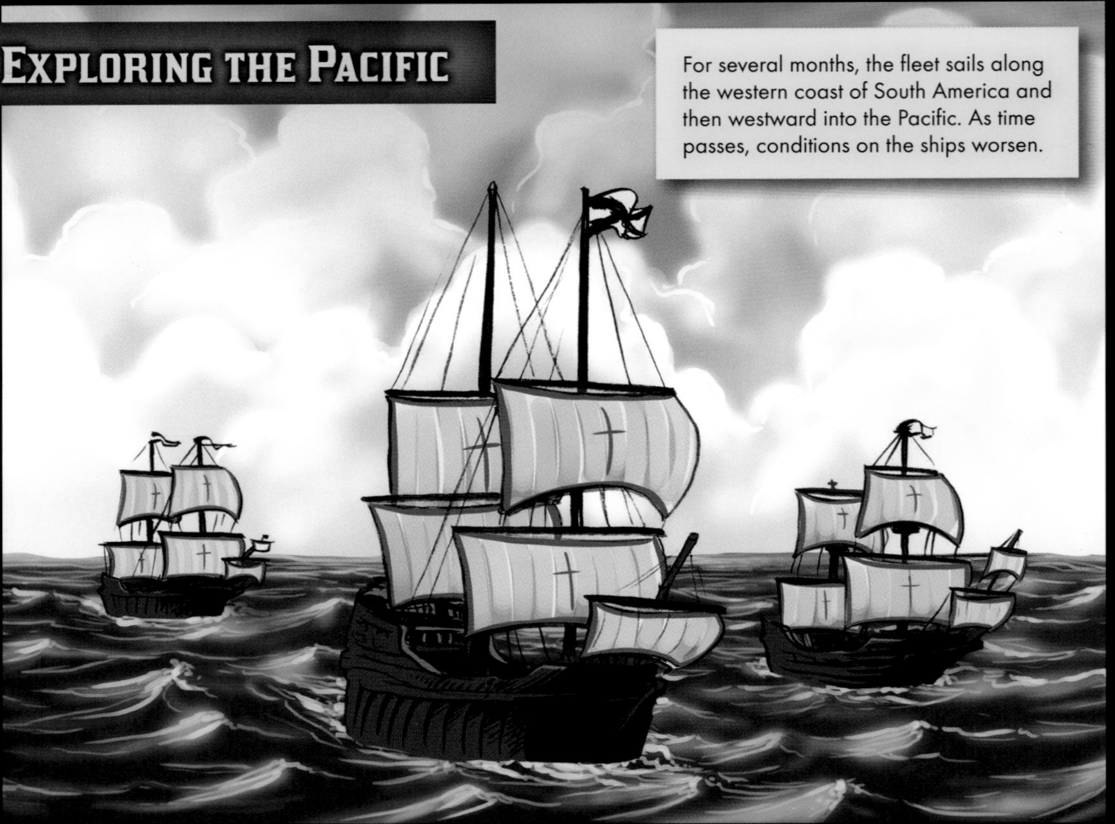
For several months, the fleet sails along the western coast of South America and then westward into the Pacific. As time passes, conditions on the ships worsen.

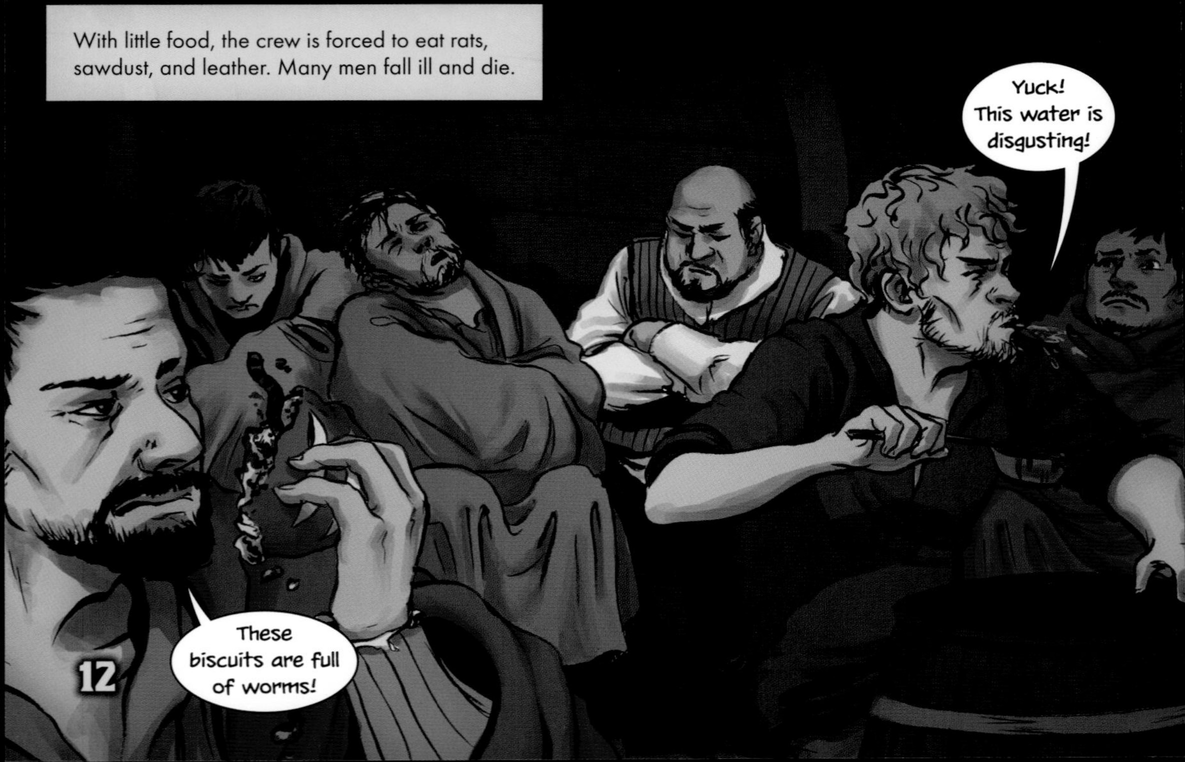
With little food, the crew is forced to eat rats, sawdust, and leather. Many men fall ill and die.
Yuck! This water is disgusting!
These biscuits are full of worms!

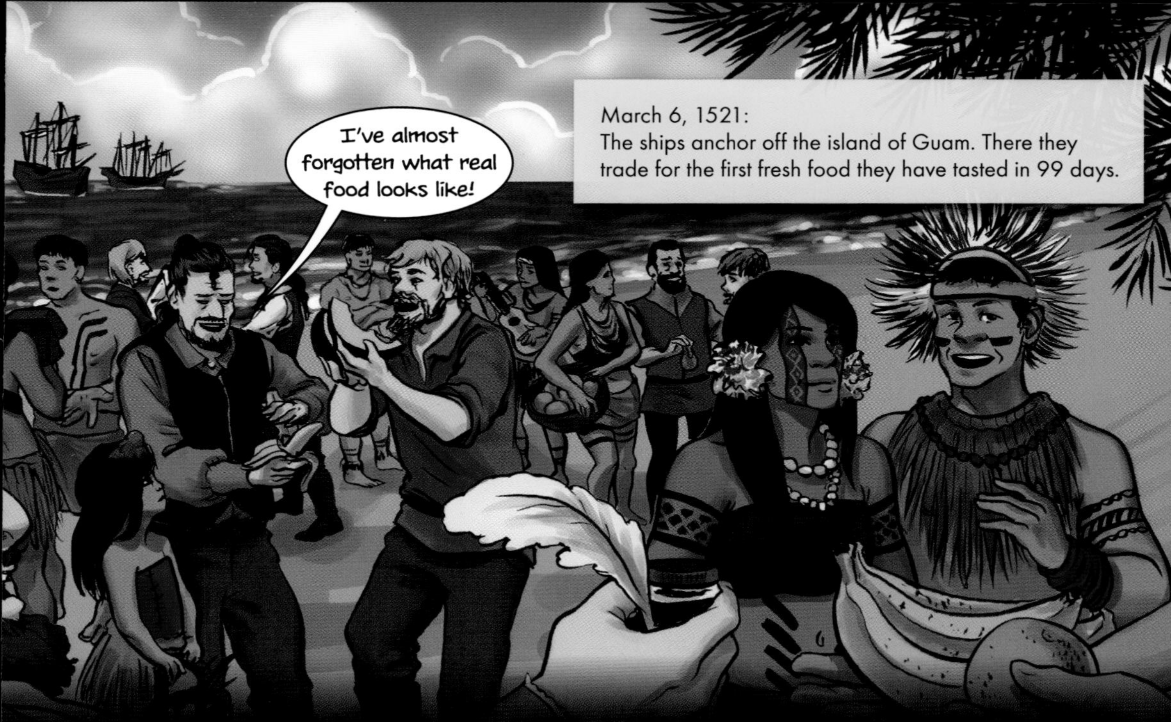
March 6, 1521:
The ships anchor off the island of Guam. There they trade for the first fresh food they have tasted in 99 days.
I've almost forgotten what real food looks like!

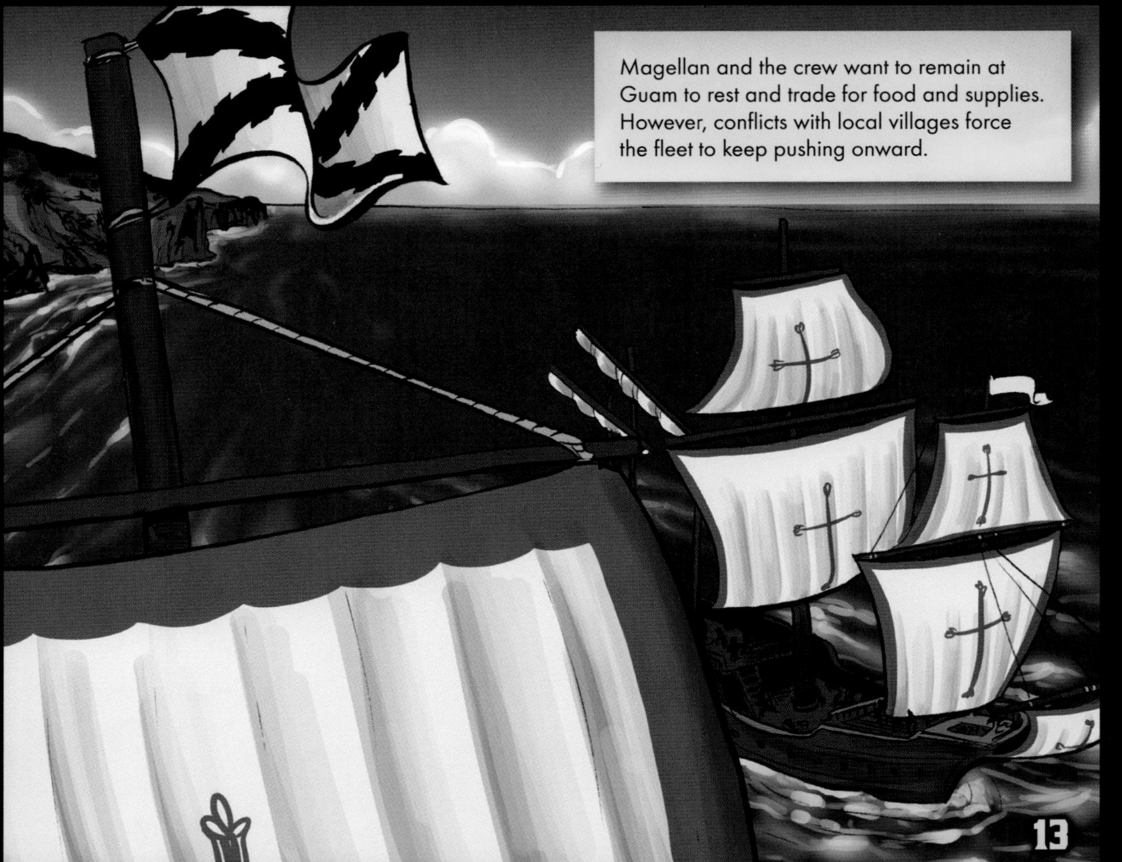
Magellan and the crew want to remain at Guam to rest and trade for food and supplies. However, conflicts with local villages force the fleet to keep pushing onward.

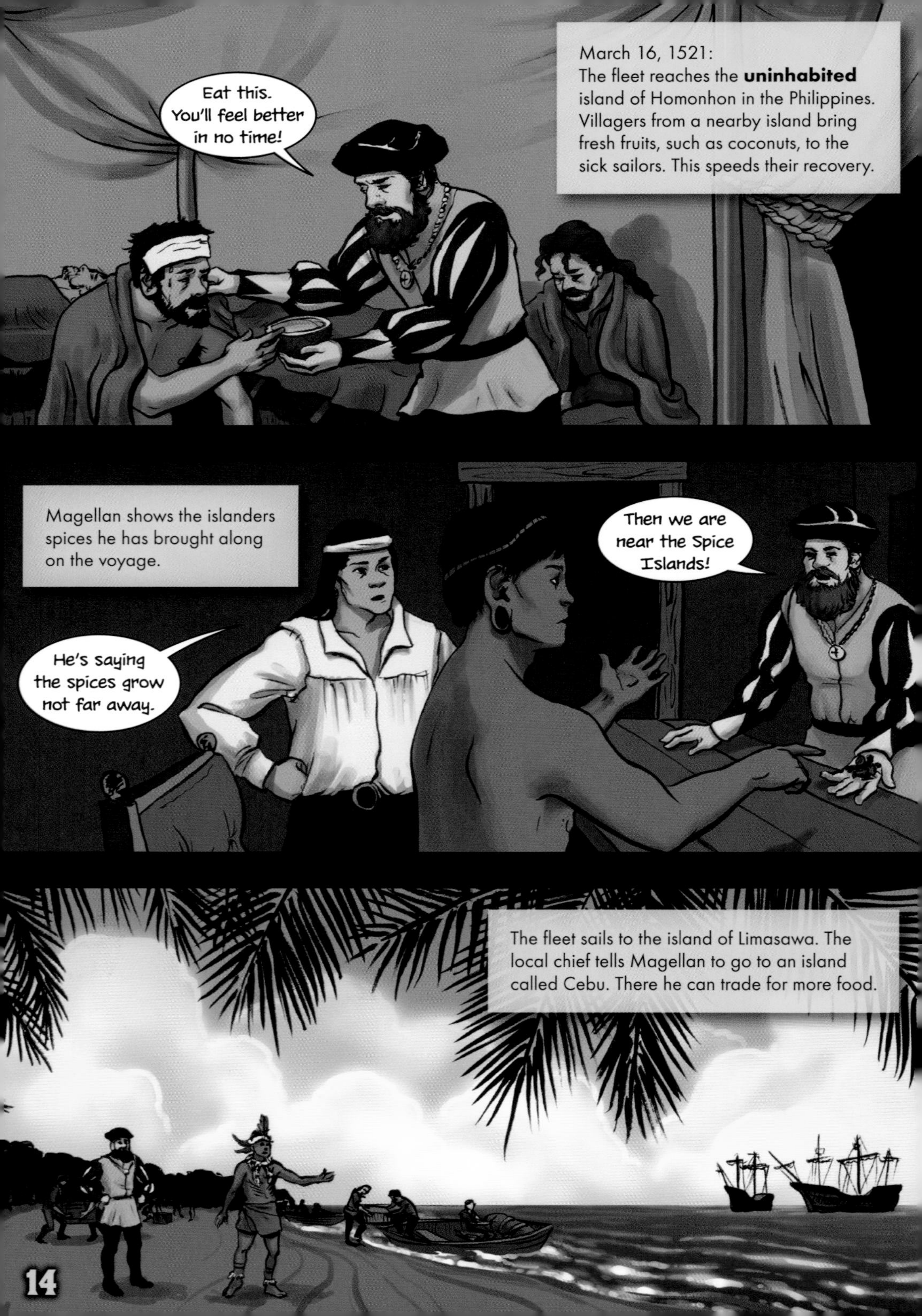
March 16, 1521:
The fleet reaches the **uninhabited** island of Homonhon in the Philippines. Villagers from a nearby island bring fresh fruits, such as coconuts, to the sick sailors. This speeds their recovery.
Eat this. You'll feel better in no time!
Magellan shows the islanders spices he has brought along on the voyage.
Then we are near the Spice Islands!
He's saying the spices grow not far away.
The fleet sails to the island of Limasawa. The local chief tells Magellan to go to an island called Cebu. There he can trade for more food.

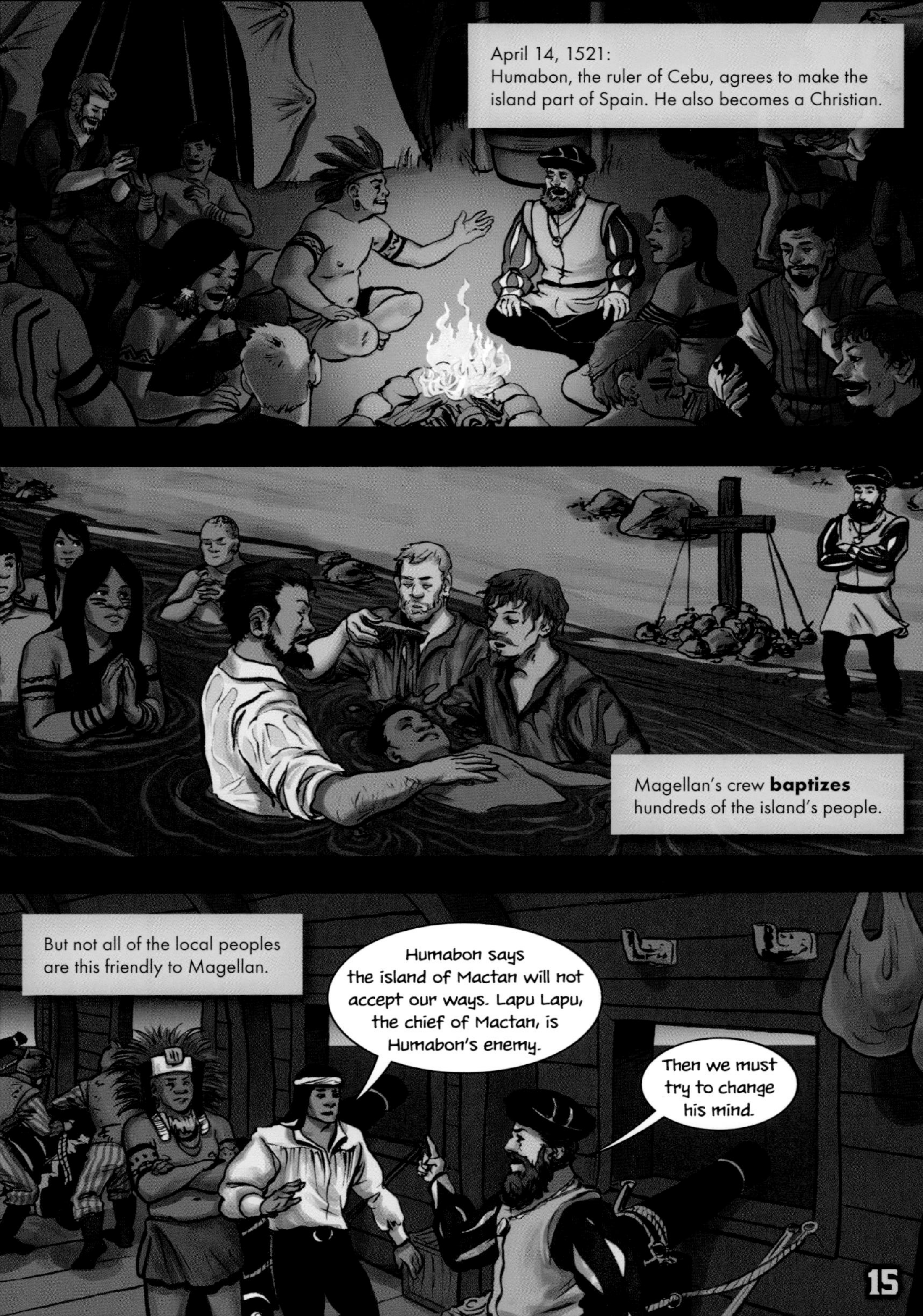
April 14, 1521:
Humabon, the ruler of Cebu, agrees to make the island part of Spain. He also becomes a Christian.
Magellan's crew **baptizes** hundreds of the island's people.
But not all of the local peoples are this friendly to Magellan.
Humabon says the island of Mactan will not accept our ways. Lapu Lapu, the chief of Mactan, is Humabon's enemy.
Then we must try to change his mind.

Disaster!

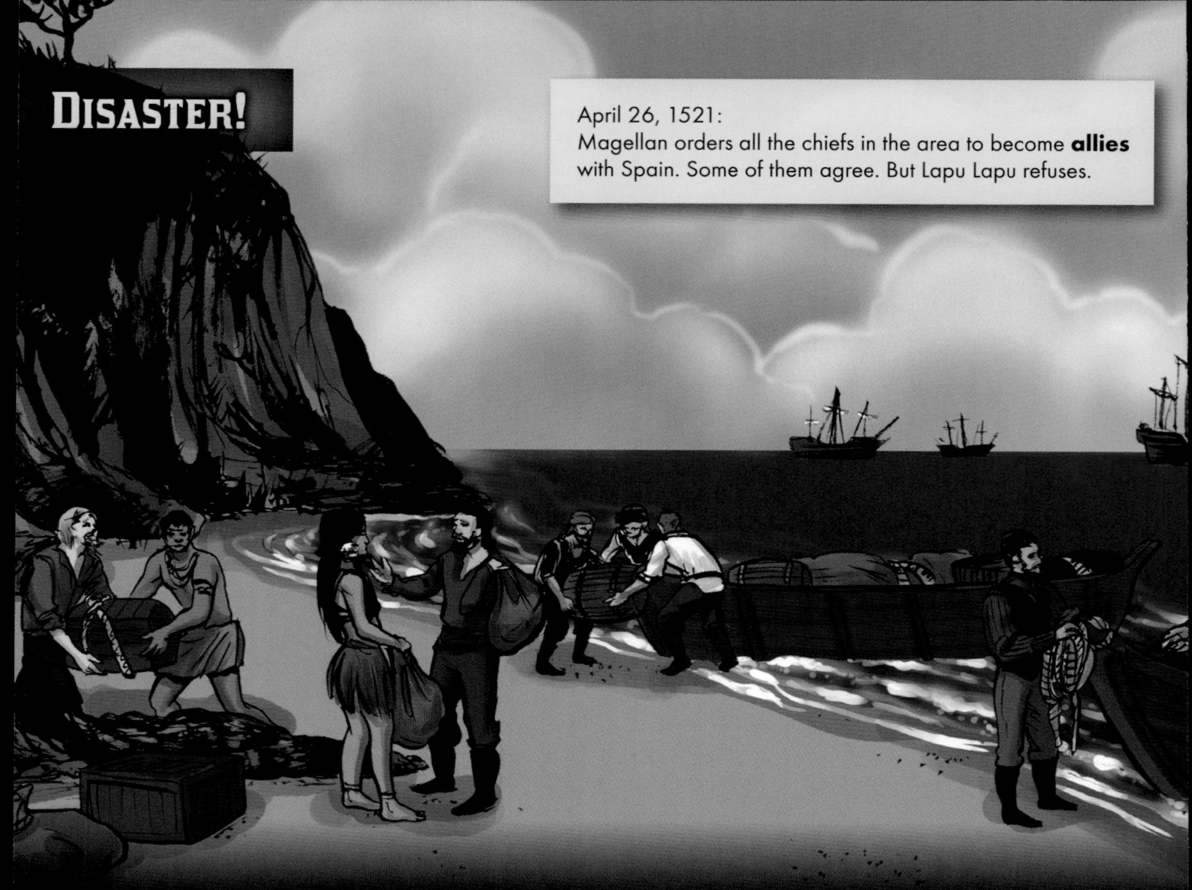
April 26, 1521:
Magellan orders all the chiefs in the area to become **allies** with Spain. Some of them agree. But Lapu Lapu refuses.

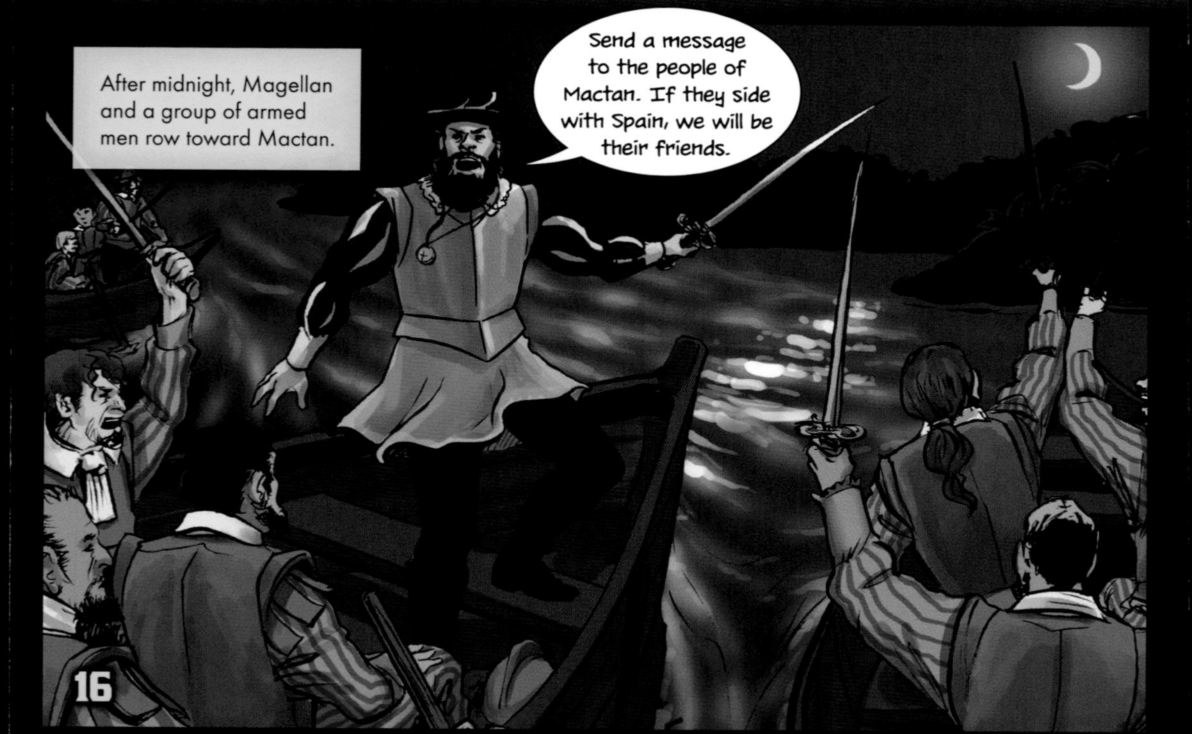
After midnight, Magellan and a group of armed men row toward Mactan.
Send a message to the people of Mactan. If they side with Spain, we will be their friends.

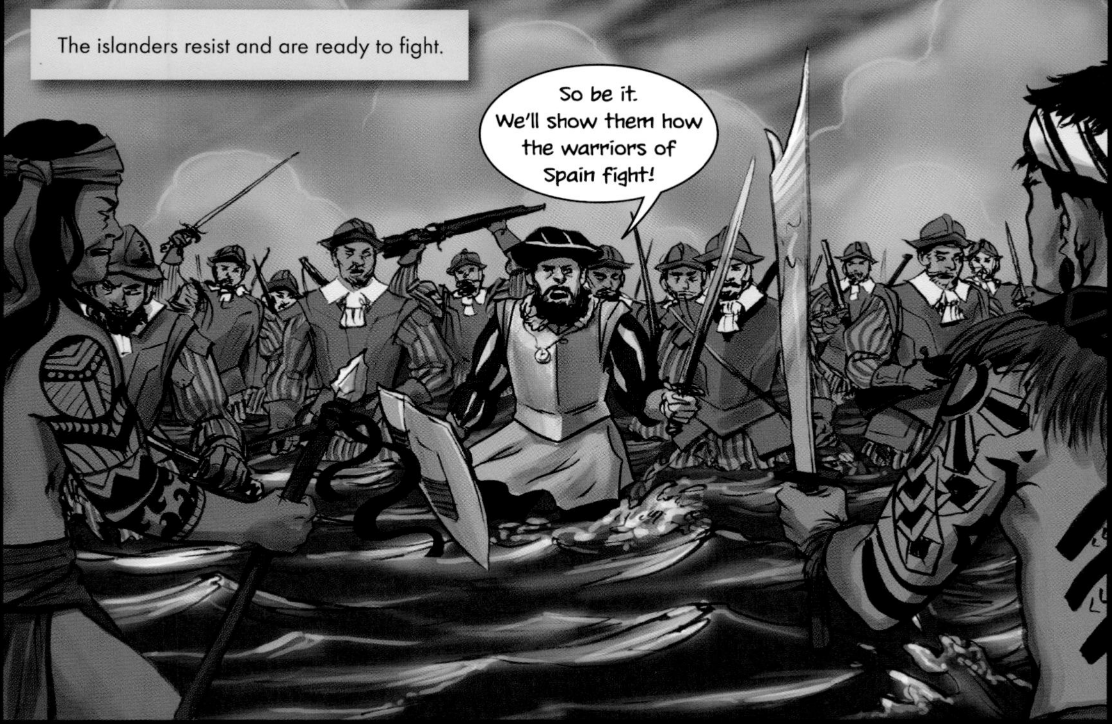
The islanders resist and are ready to fight.
So be it. We'll show them how the warriors of Spain fight!

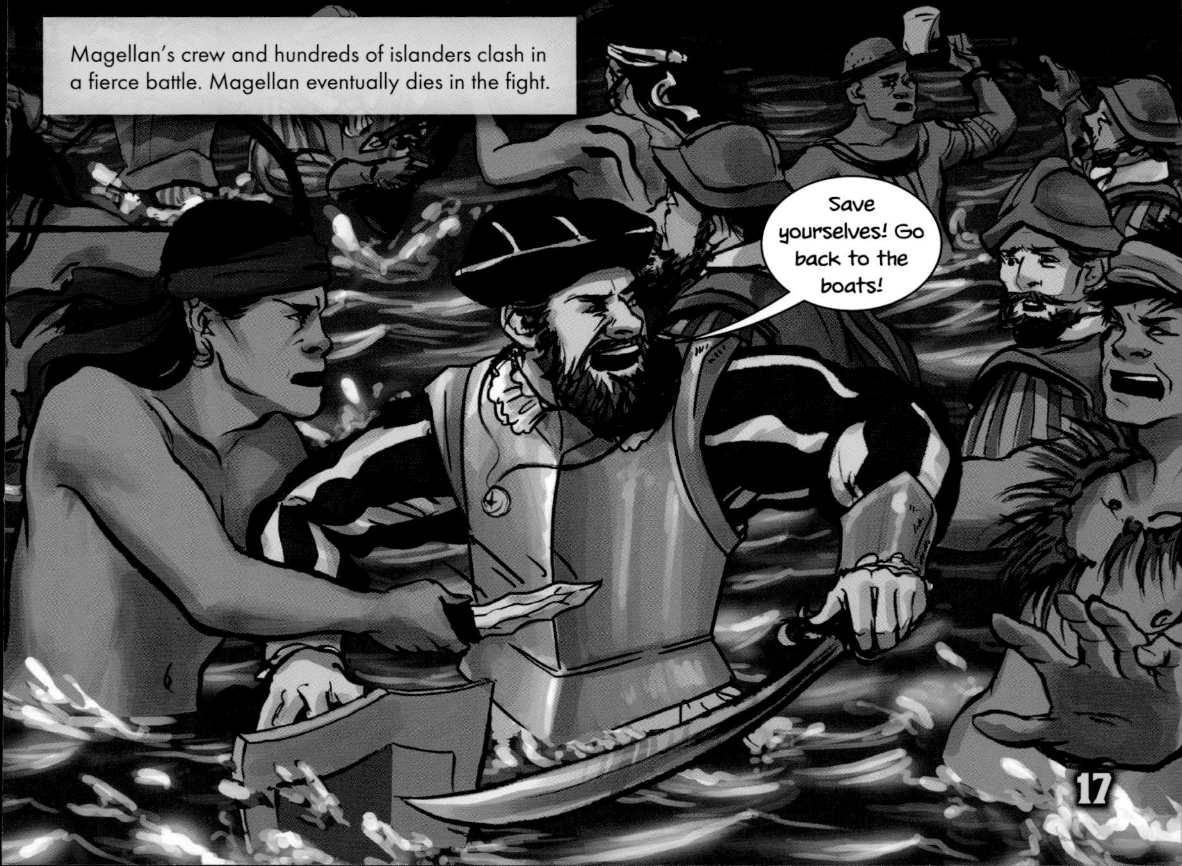
Magellan's crew and hundreds of islanders clash in a fierce battle. Magellan eventually dies in the fight.
Save yourselves! Go back to the boats!

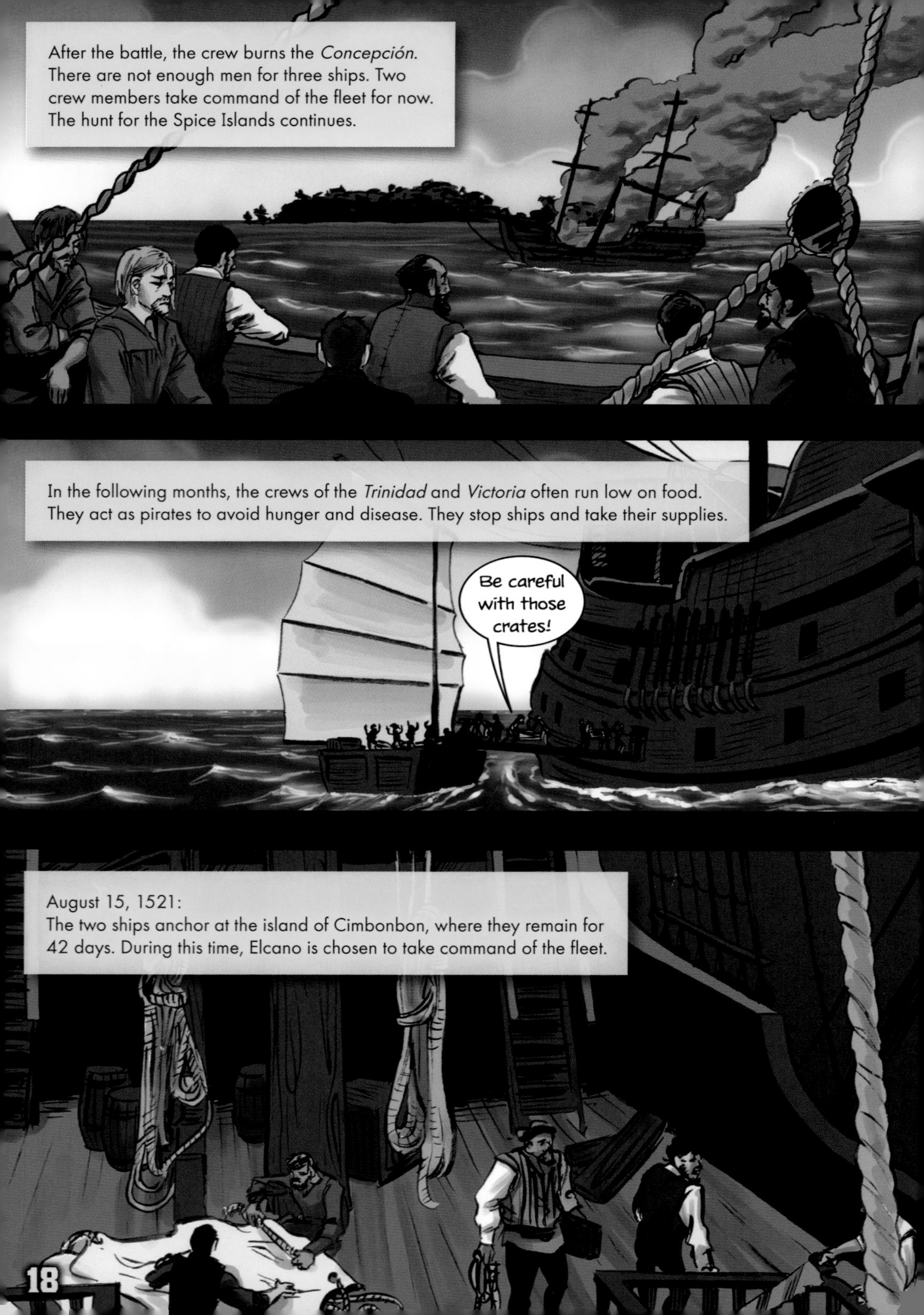
After the battle, the crew burns the *Concepción*. There are not enough men for three ships. Two crew members take command of the fleet for now. The hunt for the Spice Islands continues.
In the following months, the crews of the *Trinidad* and *Victoria* often run low on food. They act as pirates to avoid hunger and disease. They stop ships and take their supplies.
Be careful with those crates!
August 15, 1521:
The two ships anchor at the island of Cimbonbon, where they remain for 42 days. During this time, Elcano is chosen to take command of the fleet.

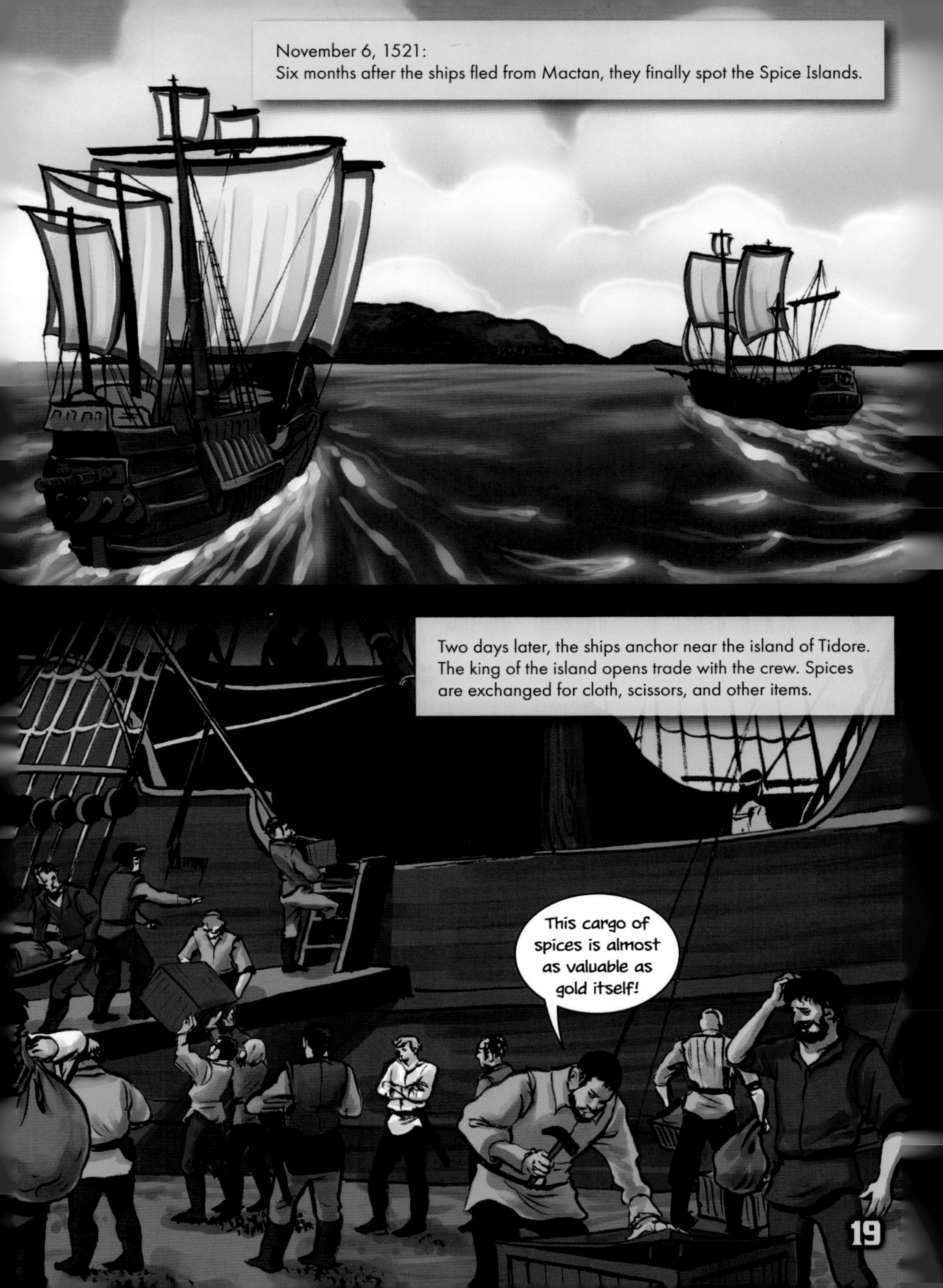
November 6, 1521:
Six months after the ships fled from Mactan, they finally spot the Spice Islands.
Two days later, the ships anchor near the island of Tidore. The king of the island opens trade with the crew. Spices are exchanged for cloth, scissors, and other items.
This cargo of spices is almost as valuable as gold itself!

Aboard the *Victoria*, Elcano discusses the return voyage to Spain with his pilot.

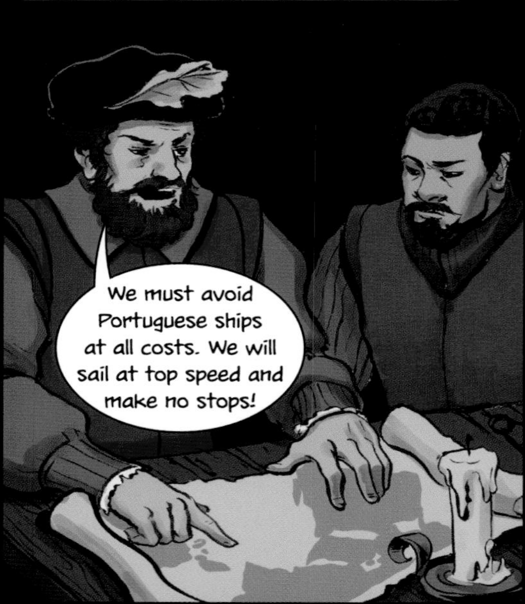
We must avoid Portuguese ships at all costs. We will sail at top speed and make no stops!

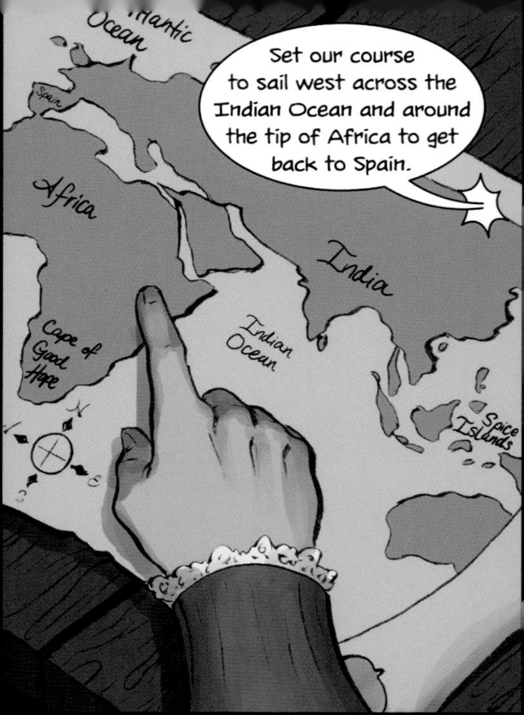
Set our course to sail west across the Indian Ocean and around the tip of Africa to get back to Spain.
Ocean
Spain
Africa
India
Cape of Good Hope
Indian Ocean
Spice Islands

The *Trinidad* develops a leak and is not fit to make the return voyage with the *Victoria*.

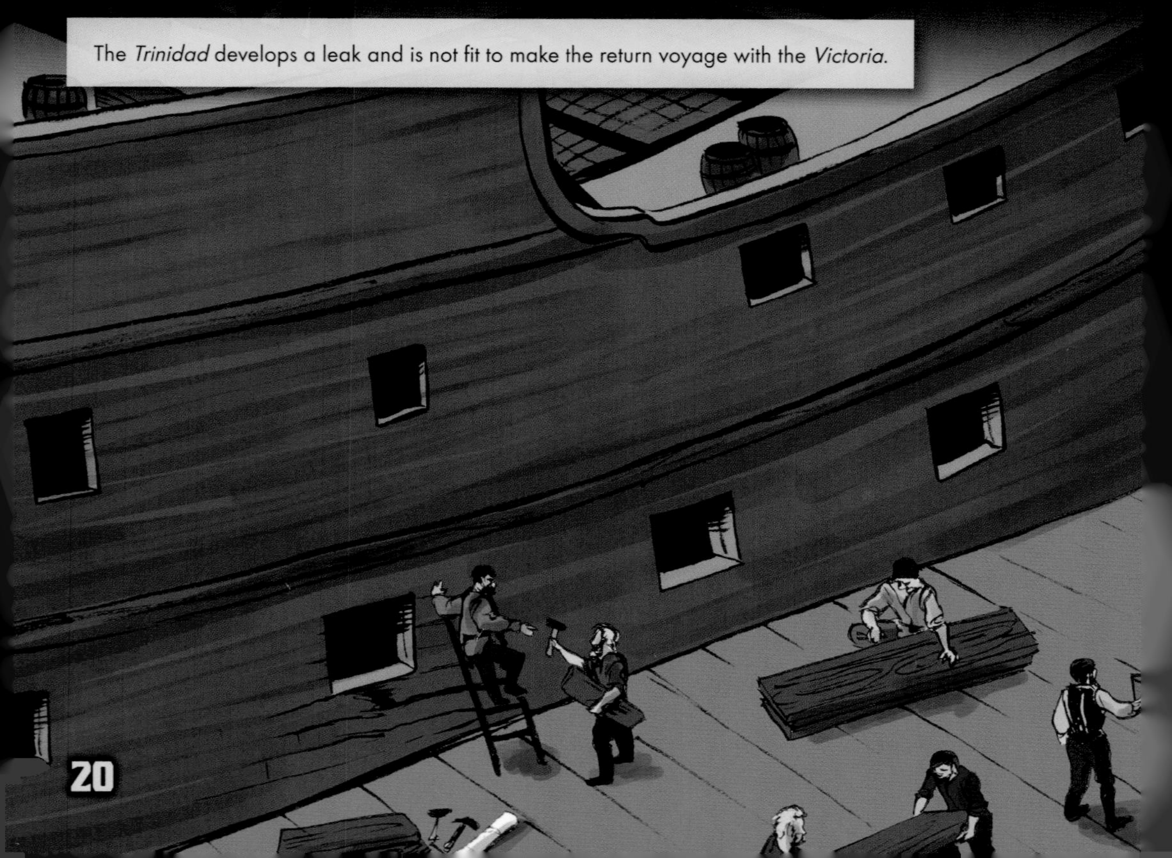

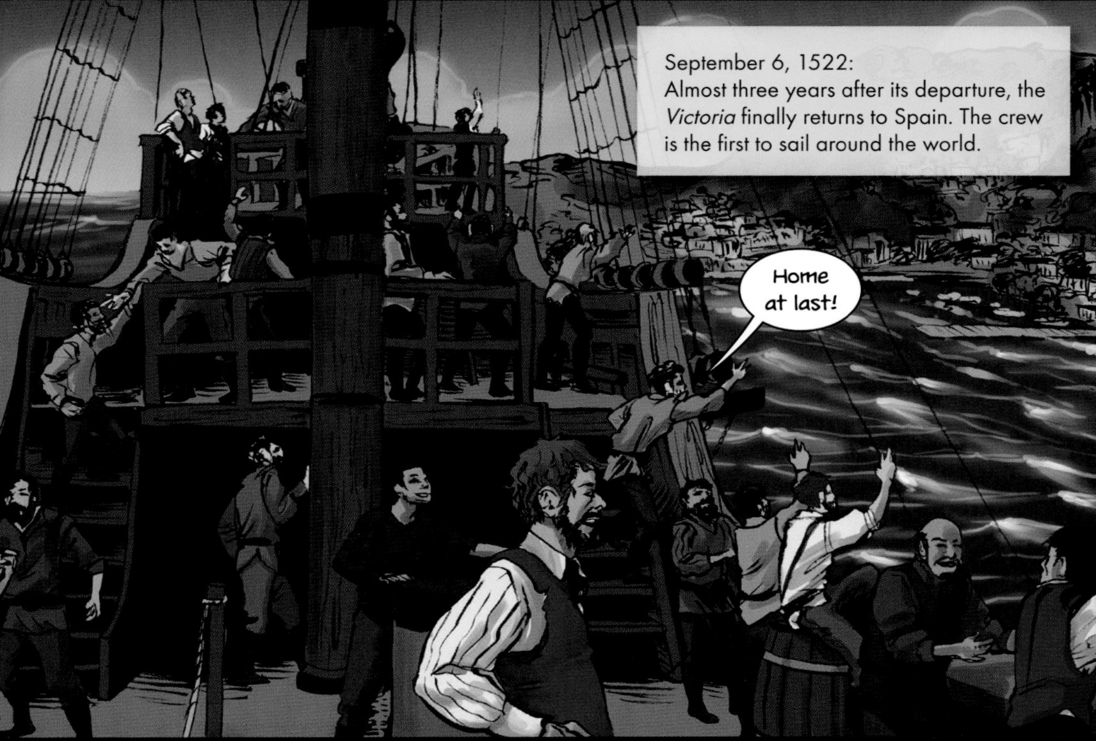
September 6, 1522:
Almost three years after its departure, the *Victoria* finally returns to Spain. The crew is the first to sail around the world.
Home at last!

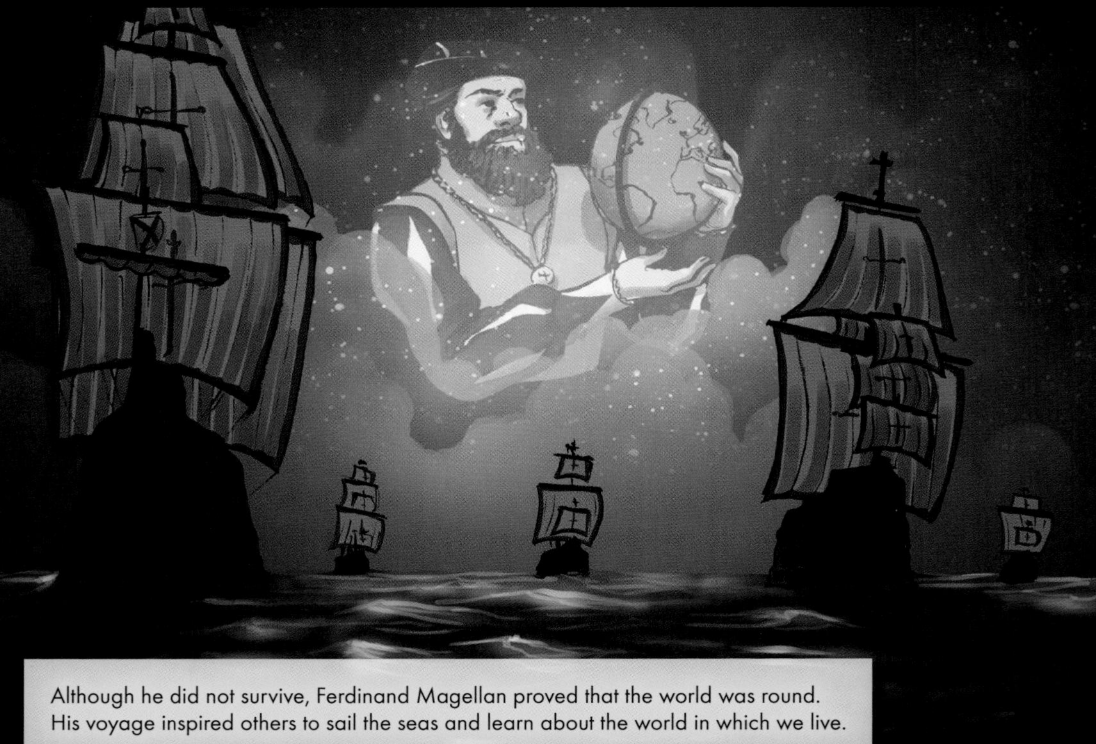
Although he did not survive, Ferdinand Magellan proved that the world was round. His voyage inspired others to sail the seas and learn about the world in which we live.

MORE ABOUT FERDINAND MAGELLAN

- Magellan's expedition included sailors from Spain, Portugal, Greece, Sicily, England, France, Germany, and North Africa.

- The caravel was the type of ship used on Magellan's expedition. Caravels were small, fast, and easy to navigate.

- Magellan's crew reported meeting 8-foot-tall (2.4-meter-tall) people on the beaches of Patagonia in present-day Argentina. Historians claim the "giants" were really not that tall.

- The route that Magellan took through the southern part of South America is now known as the Strait of Magellan. It connects the Atlantic and Pacific Oceans.

- Magellan gave the Pacific Ocean its name. He named it *Mar Pacifico*, meaning "peaceful sea" in the Portuguese language.

- Of the 270 men who sailed with Magellan in 1519, only 35 survived the journey.

Glossary

abandon—to leave with no plan to return

allies—people who are on the same side

anchored—stayed in one place in the water

baptizes—dips someone in water as a sign that he or she has become a Christian

expedition—a long trip made for a specific purpose

fleet—a group of ships under one command

inlet—a narrow body of water that leads inland from an ocean

mutiny—a revolt against the leader of a ship

rations—limited amounts of food

rebellion—a struggle against the people in charge of something

reefs—strips of rocks, sand, or coral close to the surface of the ocean

strait—a narrow strip of water that connects two larger bodies of water

uninhabited—not lived in

uprising—a revolt or rebellion

To Learn More

AT THE LIBRARY

Gould, Jane H. *Ferdinand Magellan*. New York, N.Y.: PowerKids Press, 2013.

Ollhoff, Jim. *Ferdinand Magellan*. Edina, Minn.: ABDO Publishing Company, 2014.

Powell, Marie. *Explore with Ferdinand Magellan*. New York, N.Y.: Crabtree Publishing, 2015.

ON THE WEB

Learning more about Ferdinand Magellan is as easy as 1, 2, 3.

1. Go to www.factsurfer.com.
2. Enter "Ferdinand Magellan" into the search box.
3. Click the "Surf" button and you will see a list of related web sites.

With factsurfer.com, finding more information is just a click away.

Index